DAILY PRAYERS

FOR THE
CORONATION
OF
KING CHARLES III

**FROM THE
CHURCH OF ENGLAND**

CHURCH HOUSE
PUBLISHING

Contents

About this booklet

The Coronation of King Charles III is a historic moment in the life of our nation.

The Coronation Service will take place on Saturday 6 May 2023 at Westminster Abbey, conducted by the Archbishop of Canterbury.

A ceremony rooted in longstanding tradition, the service will also reflect The King's role today and look to the future. Throughout the Coronation Weekend, themes of community life, volunteering and service will be highlighted and celebrated both nationally and locally.

To mark this important occasion, the Church of England has compiled this series of *Daily Prayers for the Coronation of King Charles III*.

Beginning on Sunday 9 April – four weeks before the Coronation – this booklet offers a prayer, a short reading and reflection on a different theme each day. It is designed to help individuals, churches or groups who wish to use these days:

- to pray for The King, The Queen Consort and the Royal Family and their calling to a life of public service
- to pray for our nation, for the Commonwealth and the family of nations of which we are a part at a time of significant change and challenge

- to learn more about the rich symbolism of the Coronation Service and its spiritual significance
- to reflect on Jesus, the Servant King, who has been crowned in glory, but who came to serve and who calls his followers to do the same.

In addition to this commemorative booklet – which also includes prayers for The King and the Royal Family for use in the months and years beyond the coronation – you can also sign up to have the daily reflections delivered free to your inbox.

You can find full details of these and other Coronation resources for individuals, churches and schools by visiting cofe.io/Coronation or by following the Church of England on social media.

Finally, the start of our daily prayers coincides with Easter Day (9 April 2023), which falls 28 days before the coronation. As we celebrate the hope of the resurrection this Easter season, we also remember before God the life of service to which our King has been called. And we pray that King Charles – and all of us – may find strength, confidence, and encouragement in the promises of Easter.

WEEK ONE

DAY 1

Called to pray

Jesus said to his disciples, 'You did not choose me but I chose you. And I appointed you to go and bear fruit, fruit that will last, so that the Father will give you whatever you ask him in my name.'

JOHN 15.16

To pray is to respond to the God who reached out to us in Jesus Christ. Praying is one of the ways we let God into our daily lives, into all that we think, say and do. That's why prayer involves us in awareness of the whole human family, its aspirations and needs, and its God-given potential.

Why the call to pray in these days leading up to the coronation? It's a way of accompanying King Charles as he responds to his calling. And it offers us a chance to pray with him that we may become more the people God is calling us to be, that all our lives may bear fruit that will last.

Eternal God and Father,
you create and redeem us by the power of your love:
guide and strengthen us by your Spirit,
that we may give ourselves in love and service
to one another and to you;
through Jesus Christ our Lord. Amen.

DAY 2

Called to service

Jesus said to his disciples, 'The greatest among you must become like the youngest, and the leader like one who serves. For who is greater, the one who is at the table or the one who serves? Is it not the one at the table? But I am among you as one who serves.'

LUKE 22.25–27

The call to service is central to our understanding of the monarchy. King Charles has already pledged himself to that vocation. Speaking just after the death of his mother Queen Elizabeth II, he made a commitment to follow the pattern of loving service that she demonstrated, a service of 'loyalty, respect, and love'.

As The King prepares for this lifelong task, we reflect on the example of Jesus, who came not to be served but to serve. Jesus shows us what we might all aspire to: the possibility of living for others, of seeking the wellbeing of the whole community, of moving beyond self-interest to self-sacrifice.

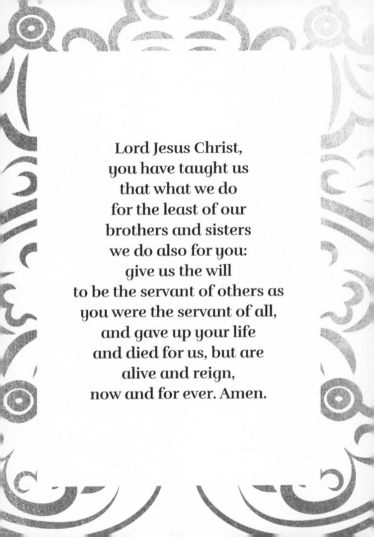

Lord Jesus Christ,
you have taught us
that what we do
for the least of our
brothers and sisters
we do also for you:
give us the will
to be the servant of others as
you were the servant of all,
and gave up your life
and died for us, but are
alive and reign,
now and for ever. Amen.

DAY 3

Called to dedication

And all of you must clothe yourselves with humility
in your dealings with one another, for 'God opposes
the proud, but gives grace to the humble.' Humble
yourselves therefore under the mighty hand of God,
so that he may exalt you in due time. Cast all your
anxiety on him, because he cares for you.

1 PETER 5.5-7

In 1947 the then Princess Elizabeth dedicated herself
to the service of the people whose queen she would
become. It was a promise she kept for the rest of her life.

For over 70 years Queen Elizabeth put duty first,
winning the love of the country as she did so. We pray
with and for our King as he strives to do the same.

Sovereign God,
who called King Charles
to be a ruler among his people:
give him grace to be their servant;
and help us, following our Saviour Christ
in the path of humble service,
to see God's kingdom set forward on earth
and to enjoy its fullness in heaven;
through Jesus Christ our Lord. Amen.

WEEK TWO

A servant king

Jesus said, 'Whoever wishes to be great among you must be your servant, and whoever wishes to be first among you must be your slave; just as the Son of Man came not to be served but to serve, and to give his life as a ransom for many.'

MATTHEW 20.26–28

Following in his mother's footsteps, King Charles' leadership is rooted in a desire and a commitment to serve, following the ways of Christ in joy-filled servant-heartedness.

As we prepare to witness the grandeur of the coronation, we pray for King Charles as, amid all the ceremony, he vows to serve his people as a servant of God. May he have the grace to lead in humility with all his heart, mind, soul and strength.

Almighty God, whose kingdom is everlasting, and power infinite: have mercy upon the whole Church; and so rule the heart of thy chosen servant Charles, our King and Governor, that he (knowing whose minister he is) may above all things seek thy honour and glory: and that we and all his subjects (duly considering whose authority he hath) may faithfully serve, honour, and humbly obey him, in thee, and for thee, according to thy blessed Word and ordinance; through Jesus Christ our Lord. Amen.

DAY 9

A symbol of the nation

Wisdom says, 'By me kings reign, and rulers decree what is just; by me rulers rule, and nobles, all who govern rightly. I love those who love me, and those who seek me diligently find me.'

PROVERBS 8.15–17

The King is Head of State of the United Kingdom. He appoints the Prime Minister and summons Parliament. But he is also an important symbol of British sovereignty. His face appears on coins and banknotes. Oaths of allegiance are made to him, and he appears as a representative of the UK in our international relations.

We pray for The King as he fulfils this important role in national and international affairs, that he may be an example of the wisdom, justice, and care that we all seek in our lives.

Almighty God,
let thy wisdom be his guide,
and let thine arm strengthen him;
let truth and justice,
holiness and righteousness,
peace and charity,
abound in his days;
direct all his counsels and endeavours
to thy glory, and the welfare of his subjects. Amen.

Head of the Commonwealth

Ascribe to the Lord, you families of the peoples;
ascribe to the Lord honour and strength ...

O worship the Lord in the beauty of holiness;
let the whole earth tremble before him.

PSALM 96.7,9

The Commonwealth (or Commonwealth of Nations) is a unique grouping of 56 developed and developing nations, comprising 30 per cent of the world's population spread across a quarter of the world's land mass on every continent. Many members were once part of the British Empire.

The modern Commonwealth was born in 1949 when India, on gaining independence and republican status, agreed to remain in the Commonwealth based on 'free association' and 'equality', with the British Monarch becoming 'a symbol of the free association of independent members nations, and as such, Head of the Commonwealth'.

The King heads this 'family of nations' which seeks to enrich the life of its members and the world through shared values and practical cooperation. It's an ambitious goal, for which we need to pray.

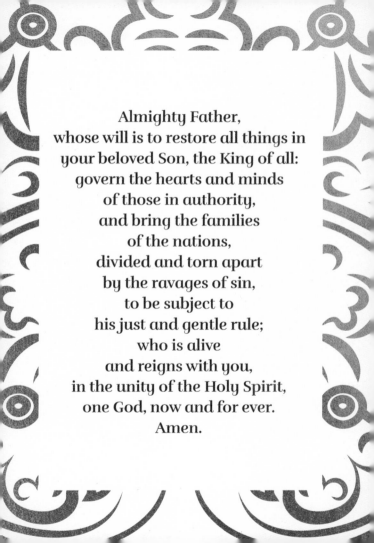

Almighty Father,
whose will is to restore all things in
your beloved Son, the King of all:
govern the hearts and minds
of those in authority,
and bring the families
of the nations,
divided and torn apart
by the ravages of sin,
to be subject to
his just and gentle rule;
who is alive
and reigns with you,
in the unity of the Holy Spirit,
one God, now and for ever.
Amen.

Part of the Anglican Communion

You are a chosen race, a holy nation, God's own people, in order that you may proclaim the mighty acts of him who called you out of darkness into his marvellous light.

1 PETER 2.9

Although its spread reaches well beyond the Commonwealth, the Anglican Communion is, like that organization, a free association of independent bodies.

The Anglican Communion comprises over forty different churches around the world, representing tens of millions of Christians. Sharing one faith in Jesus Christ, the autonomous churches of the Communion are also committed to interdependence. They strive to work together as part of the worldwide Church of Christ, 'God's own people', across the cultural differences and theological disagreements which mark their life together.

We pray that our King, Supreme Governor of the Church of England, may encourage us in this quest for unity.

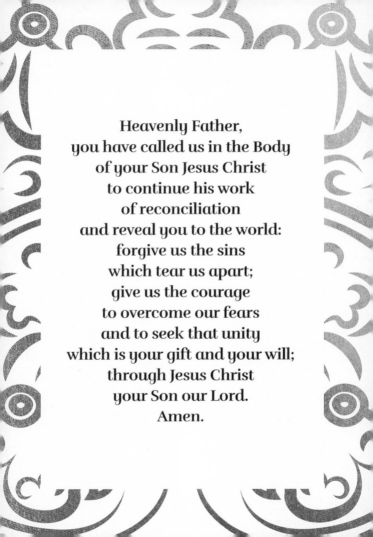

Heavenly Father,
you have called us in the Body
of your Son Jesus Christ
to continue his work
of reconciliation
and reveal you to the world:
forgive us the sins
which tear us apart;
give us the courage
to overcome our fears
and to seek that unity
which is your gift and your will;
through Jesus Christ
your Son our Lord.
Amen.

DAY 12

Westminster Abbey

I was glad when they said unto me,
'We will go into the house of the Lord.'
PSALM 122.1

Westminster Abbey was founded by King Edward the Confessor and consecrated just before his death in 1066. Edward was revered as a saintly king, and ever since our monarchs have knelt in prayer at his tomb in the Abbey before their coronation.

Today we think of the ideal of the king, and those who govern in his name: that in their personal and public lives they may show the values of God's kingdom, where those in need are cared for and the oppressed lifted up, and there is peace and justice between people and nations. We pray for strength to live as citizens of the kingdom where God reigns.

Sovereign God,
who set your servant Edward
upon the throne of an earthly kingdom
and inspired him with zeal
for the kingdom of heaven:
grant that we may so confess the faith of Christ
by word and deed,
that we may, with all your saints,
inherit your eternal glory;
through Jesus Christ our Lord. Amen.

DAY 13

Praying for the Holy Spirit

*Jesus breathed on the disciples and said to them,
'Receive the Holy Spirit.'*

JOHN 20.22

The 1625 coronation of King Charles I used a translation of the Latin hymn to the Holy Spirit, *Veni, Creator Spiritus* (Come, Holy Spirit) by John Cosin. This beautiful text has been sung at every coronation since then.

And after it was included in the 1662 Book of Common Prayer, it came to be included in services of confirmation and ordination as we recall the royal priesthood in which we all participate. It prays that we may live always within the breath of Jesus Christ, receiving life from him, so that he may inspire in us authentic life, the life that death can never take away.

Come, Holy Ghost, our souls inspire,
And lighten with celestial fire.
Thou the anointing Spirit art,
Who dost thy seven-fold gifts impart.

Anoint and cheer our soiled face
With the abundance of thy grace:
Keep far our foes, give peace at home;
Where thou art guide, no ill can come.

Anointed with oil

The spirit of the Lord God is upon me, because the Lord has anointed me; he has sent me to bring good news to the oppressed, to bind up the broken-hearted, to proclaim liberty to the captives, and release to the prisoners; to proclaim the year of the Lord's favour.

ISAIAH 61.1-2

At the heart of the coronation is a ritual in which the Archbishop of Canterbury anoints The King with oil. This custom, with roots in the Old Testament, can be traced back to the coronation of King Edgar by St Dunstan in 973. At this coronation, the oil will come from the Mount of Olives in Jerusalem where The King's grandmother, Princess Alice of Battenberg, is buried.

The outward and visible act of anointing signifies an inward grace: we pray that God would bless and set apart King Charles to serve the people of our nation and Commonwealth with humility and joy. The words of Isaiah, adopted by Jesus himself at the start of his ministry, will be an inspiration.

**Almighty God,
send down upon your Church
the riches of your Spirit,
and kindle in all who minister the gospel
your countless gifts of grace;
through Jesus Christ our Lord. Amen.**

WEEK THREE

The Coronation Regalia

What are mortals, that you should be mindful of them;
mere human beings, that you should seek them out?

You have made them little lower than the angels
and crown them with glory and honour.

PSALM 8.5,6

For over a thousand years our kings and queens have been invested with ring, sceptre, rod, orb and crown. These golden objects are adorned with diamonds and other precious stones, worldly wealth beyond measure.

And yet the ring is marked with a cross, and the other objects are each topped with one, symbolizing the authority of Christ. A dove, the symbol of God the Holy Spirit, perches on the cross at the top of the rod. Together they remind us that Jesus Christ is king over all. Christ reigns from the cross, wearing a crown of thorns, defying the world's expectations, forgiving and loving to the end, dying and rising that we might have life in all its fullness.

God the Father,
help us to hear the call of Christ the King
and to follow in his service,
whose kingdom has no end;
for he reigns with you and the Holy Spirit,
one God, one glory. Amen.

The National Anthem

Then they blew the trumpet, and all the people
said, 'Long live King Solomon!' And all the people
went up following him, playing on pipes
and rejoicing with great joy, so that the earth
quaked at their noise.

1 KINGS 1.39,40

We hear the National Anthem so often in different
situations: at sporting fixtures, at civic, military, and
community occasions, and on television and radio.
Some people may remember a time when it was
played in theatres and cinemas. When we take a
moment to listen to the words and consider what
they mean, we may be surprised to recall that it is,
at its heart, a prayer for the Sovereign.

As we sing, we pray to God that he might protect
and care for our King, that God will grant him good
things, happiness, and long life as he serves us.

God save our gracious King!
Long live our noble King!
God save the King!
Send him victorious,
Happy and glorious,
Long to reign over us,
God save the King.

DAY 19

Love

Jesus said, 'I give you a new commandment,
that you love one another. Just as I have loved you,
you also should love one another.'

JOHN 13.34

In her 1975 Christmas broadcast, the late Queen
reflected on the value and importance of our
relationships and love of one another. She said,
'[Christ] commanded us to love our neighbours as
we love ourselves, but what exactly is meant by
"loving ourselves"? I believe it means trying to make
the most of the abilities we have been given, it
means caring for our talents.'

The Bible can be read as a narrative of God's love,
and of how we can imitate that love in the way we
live. St Paul's Letter to the Galatians speaks of nine
qualities given to those who are guided by the
Holy Spirit: the so-called 'Fruit of the Spirit'. Love is
the first of these, and all the others (which we will
be exploring in the coming days) are expressions
or outcomes of love.

We pray that King Charles will, throughout his reign,
continue to know God's love and to abide in that love
as he fulfills his responsibilities.

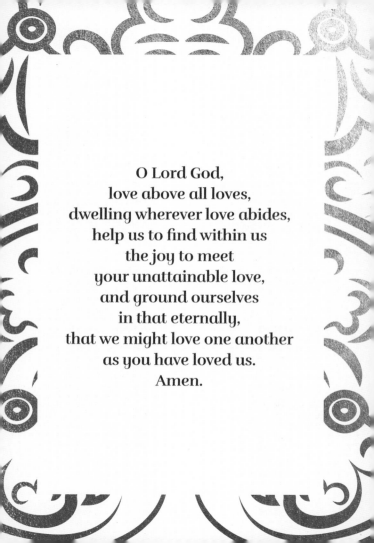

O Lord God,
love above all loves,
dwelling wherever love abides,
help us to find within us
the joy to meet
your unattainable love,
and ground ourselves
in that eternally,
that we might love one another
as you have loved us.
Amen.

DAY 20

Joy

Jesus said, 'If you keep my commandments, you
will abide in my love, just as I have kept my Father's
commandments and abide in his love. I have said
these things to you so that my joy may be in you,
and that your joy may be complete.'

JOHN 15.10,11

The life of our King will be marked, like all our lives,
with a balance of pleasure and hardship, of delight
and challenge. Experiencing joy in all things can be
difficult for anyone. But joy goes much deeper than
happiness or cheerfulness. It is a rootedness in joyful
love of God and those around us. It has the power to
uplift the soul even amid life's pain and challenges.

As King Charles prepares for his coronation, we pray
with him that he may continually seek, find, and
radiate joy in all things.

Eternal God, author of all joyfulness
and the music of our dance,
may the joy that is yours echo in our hearts.
May it shine through us, glowing with faith,
uplifting our souls heavenward,
as we abide in your hope and love. Amen.

DAY 21

Peace

Jesus said to his disciples, 'Peace I leave with you;
my peace I give to you.'

JOHN 14.27

'Peace' is the word most often used to translate the Hebrew word *shalom*, which appears 250 times in the Old Testament. Surely a word used so often conveys so much more than what might be called 'an absence of war'.

The Hebrew *shalom* communicates at its heart a sense of total harmony. Even inanimate objects could be in *shalom*. For example, when King Solomon finished all the work on the Temple, it was in *shalom* (1 Kings 7.51). Later, the prophet Zechariah declared, 'Your king will make *shalom* among the nations' (Zechariah 9.16).

In these days of prayer, let us pray that our nation under The King may hold fast to the promise of peace.

God our Saviour,
look on this wounded world in pity and in power;
hold us fast to your promises of peace
won for us by your Son,
our Saviour Jesus Christ. Amen.

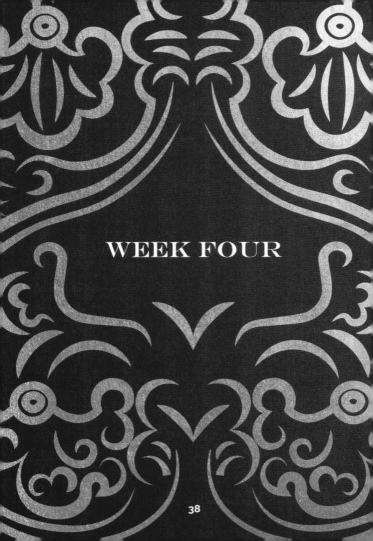

WEEK FOUR

DAY 22

Patience

I waited patiently for the Lord;
he inclined to me and heard my cry.

PSALM 40.1

We have all been reminded to be patient many times throughout our lives. Living in patience and peace with one another is not always easy, and is a discipline that, appropriately, takes much practice to cultivate.

Nevertheless, patience is among the Fruit of the Spirit listed by St Paul, and something we should aim to embrace whenever we can, looking to God who remains ever patient with us. All Christian people are also called to be patient and persistent in prayer.

Let us ask God for this gift today.

Lord of heaven and earth,
as Jesus taught his disciples to be persistent in prayer,
give us patience and courage never to lose hope,
but always to bring our prayers before you;
through Jesus Christ our Lord. Amen.

Kindness

What does the Lord require of you
but to do justice, and to love kindness,
and to walk humbly with your God?

MICAH 6.8

One of the phrases that is attributed to St David of
Wales is his encouragement to his community to
'be joyful, keep the faith, and do the little things that
you have seen and heard with me'. They remind us
that every instant of our lives affords an opportunity
to be drawn closer to the God who loves us, and that
small steps of kindness are indications of the Spirit
at work in our lives.

The life of service to which King Charles is dedicated
displays on the public stage the values of love and
kindness that each of us can demonstrate through what
the poet Wordsworth describes as 'little, nameless,
unremembered acts / Of kindness and of love'.

Almighty God,
who sent your Holy Spirit
to be the life and light of your Church:
open our hearts to the riches of your grace,
that we may bring forth the fruit of the Spirit
in love and joy and peace;
through Jesus Christ our Lord. Amen.

DAY 24

Generosity

God loves a cheerful giver. And God is able to
provide you with every blessing in abundance, so
that by always having enough of everything, you
may share abundantly in every good work.

2 Corinthians 9.7,8

Generosity is a joyful activity. Often generosity is a
response of gratitude, when we offer ourselves and
our resources to something we care about or believe
in. An act of giving in whatever form expresses love
and brings hope. As beings made in the image of
God, generosity is in our nature as well. We are
called to be imitators of Christ whose life was itself
a gift of self-giving love.

All of us have something to give. And there is beauty
in the simple action of giving which speaks volumes
beyond the act itself, because it comes from the heart.

God of grace,
mould us in your image
and give us a spirit of generosity
that seeks nothing but to give,
nothing but to serve,
and offers our hearts,
our whole selves to you,
the giver of all things. Amen.

DAY 25

Faithfulness

The steadfast love of the Lord never ceases,
his mercies never come to an end;
they are new every morning;
great is your faithfulness.
LAMENTATIONS 3.22,23

Our efforts to walk before God in faithfulness and uprightness of living are rooted in our response to God who, in spite of our waywardness, is faithful towards us. 'Great is thy faithfulness,' the old hymn puts it, drawing on words from Lamentations.

In the Coronation Service, the King's Oath declares that he will 'cause Law and Justice, in Mercy, to be executed in all [his] judgements'. This theme runs like a silver thread through the ceremony.

As we pray with King Charles that God will guide him in these great responsibilities, we also think of our own desire to remain faithful to God's will for us.

Lord of all power and might,
the author and giver of all good things:
graft in our hearts the love of your name,
increase in us true religion,
nourish us with all goodness,
and of your great mercy keep us in the same;
through Jesus Christ our Lord. Amen.

DAY 26

Gentleness

Jesus said, 'Come to me, all you that are weary and are carrying heavy burdens, and I will give you rest. Take my yoke upon you, and learn from me; for I am gentle and humble in heart, and you will find rest for your souls.'

MATTHEW 11.28,29

There must be very few people who can appreciate the heavy burden that being Sovereign brings. And of course the burden can only be carried by one individual at a time. Before his accession The King had been readying himself for the burden of kingship for many years.

As The King prepares for his coronation, we pray that he and The Queen Consort may know the presence of God and be supported by God's Spirit. In our reading today Jesus refers to himself as 'gentle and humble in heart'. In him, The King, The Queen Consort – and indeed all of us who bear heavy burdens – will find rest for our souls.

Tender God,
gentle protector in time of trouble,
pierce the gloom of despair and give us,
with all your people,
the song of freedom and the shout of praise;
in Jesus Christ our Lord. Amen.

DAY 27

Self-control

God did not give us a spirit of cowardice, but rather
a spirit of power and of love and of self-control.

2 TIMOTHY 1.7

Jesus offers us a wonderful example of self-control. Despite his own human fears – shown most clearly in the Garden of Gethsemane – he offered himself so that we might have eternal life.

In all circumstances of life we are all called to self-control. As we remember the important tasks set before our King, and the challenges he will face, we pray that the fruit of self-control, which informs all our actions and decisions, will give him patience and strength to act always in love and obedience to God and in service to others.

Eternal God,
give us insight
to discern your will for us,
to give up what harms us,
and to seek the perfection we are promised
in Jesus Christ our Lord. Amen.

Praying for God's help

O God, make speed to save me;
O Lord, make haste to help me.

PSALM 70.1

This appeal in the Psalms for God's assistance has been at the centre of Christian prayer for centuries. It is a good prayer to pray on waking up, on being assigned a difficult task, or when in particular need. We are always in need of God's assistance, whatever our endeavour.

As we pray with The King on this Coronation Day, let us also remember that all that we have, and all that we are, comes from the love of God.

We pray that we may always hear and strive to take up God's invitation to be with him in our lives, and that we, together with The King, may receive grace to carry out what we are called to do.

Remember, O Lord,
what you have wrought in us
and not what we deserve,
and as you have called us to your service,
so make us worthy of our calling,
through Jesus Christ our Lord. Amen.

Celebrating Community

Behold how good and pleasant it is
to dwell together in unity.

PSALM 133.1

Being part of a community is essential to human life. We find community in our friendships, families, colleagues and classmates, the places we live, and in our churches. Living in community helps shape our character and behaviours, and as a community of God we find our identity in how we grow in our faith together.

Being a community of God is also about being a community of love, belonging and togetherness. As we learn to see the nature of God in the face of others, our communities in turn reflect God's character to the world.

Many communities will have planned street parties, church services, and other celebrations for this Coronation weekend. We pray that in these occasions we, with King Charles, may recognize the face of Christ in those with whom we share them.

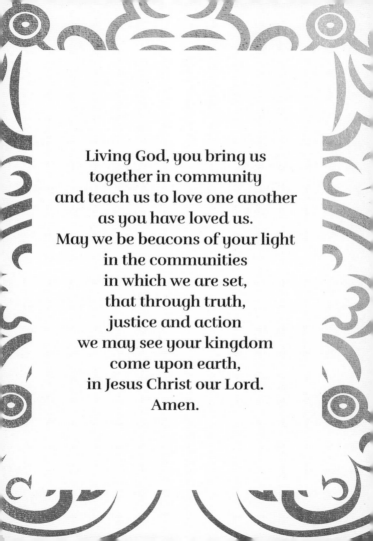

Living God, you bring us
together in community
and teach us to love one another
as you have loved us.
May we be beacons of your light
in the communities
in which we are set,
that through truth,
justice and action
we may see your kingdom
come upon earth,
in Jesus Christ our Lord.
Amen.

A Prayer for The King

Almighty God, the fountain of all goodness,
bless our Sovereign Lord, King Charles,
and all who are in authority under him;
that they may order all things
in wisdom and equity, righteousness and peace,
to the honour of your name,
and the good of your Church and people;
through Jesus Christ our Lord.
Amen.

A Prayer for the Royal Family

Almighty God, the fountain of all goodness,
bless, we pray, Camilla the Queen Consort,
William Prince of Wales, the Princess of Wales,
and all the Royal Family.
Endue them with your Holy Spirit;
enrich them with your heavenly grace;
prosper them with all happiness;
and bring them to your everlasting kingdom;
through Jesus Christ our Lord.
Amen.